vegan
cook book
For Beginners

VEGAN COOKBOOK FOR BEGINNERS

Delicious & Simple Calorie Counted Vegan Recipes

ISBN 978-1-913005-09-2
Images under licence from Shutterstock

DISCLAIMER

CONTENTS

DINNER   49

DESSERTS   71

SNACKS   87

VEGAN
FOOD

INTRODUCTION

Calorie counted vegan recipes specifically designed to help with weight loss and the maintenance of your ideal weight, while paying attention to the unique nutritional needs of vegans.

WHAT IS A VEGAN? The UK Vegan Society describes veganism as:

> *"a philosophy and way of living which seeks to exclude—as far as is possible and practicable—all forms of exploitation of, and cruelty to, animals for food, clothing or any other purpose; and by extension, promotes the development and use of animal-free alternatives for the benefit of humans, animals and the environment. In dietary terms it denotes the practice of dispensing with all products derived wholly or partly from animals."*

The word vegan first appeared in the Oxford English dictionary supplement in 1986, more than forty years after its first known use in the formation of the Vegan Society. However, although the term vegan was coined in 1944, there have been vegans and vegan diets around for a lot longer. They just used to be called vegetarians. They ate only plant-derived foods - often raw - and excluded animal-derived products from their diets and way of life.

However, as the popularity of the movement grew, it came to include people who didn't eat meat, but who did eat eggs and dairy products. The Vegan Society was formed from the stricter element within the broader Vegetarian Society and began with a mere twenty-five members. This was 1944, a time of war and food rationing, so the difficulties of these committed vegans should not be underestimated. For vegans who struggle today with finding the right nutrition, imagine doing so with food shortages and only a strict quantity of vegetables, nuts and fruits allowed. The Vegan Society tried and failed to be allowed to substitute extra nut rations for the egg, milk and cheese rations they never used.

After the war, the Vegan Society grew slowly and gradually, up until the 1970s when membership suddenly took off. The increased interest in veganism which this implies was partly due – in the UK at least - to a documentary, A Better Future for All Life, shown on the BBC in 1976. This brought the principles and benefits of veganism to a much wider audience at a time when concern for the environment in general was on the rise.

Since the 1940s, veganism has come a long way. From the days when the only non-dairy milk available in Britain was expensive coconut milk imported from America, we now have a wide selection of affordable foods labelled as suitable for vegans, and it is comparatively easy to stock our cupboards with vegan-appropriate nutrition. Many mainstream restaurant menus have vegan as well as vegetarian options.

WHAT DO VEGANS EAT?
Vegans are often described in terms of what they don't eat! Like vegetarians, they don't eat meat, but for vegans, this is the only the beginning. Any food which is produced from a live or dead animal is off the table. So, eggs, milk, butter, cheese, yogurt etc, are all taboo, as are any food stuffs made with any such ingredient. For, although eggs and dairy products do not kill the animal they're taken from, they are seen as exploiting the animals, which are made to suffer for humans. Consider, for example, the plight of battery chickens, or the cow who loses her calf to the slaughter house and is then forced to supply milk for the rest of her life before facing the slaughter house herself. And then, any animal kept to feed us, has to be fed itself, thus using up valuable resources.

Likewise, although there is some debate on the issue, honey is seen as exploitative of the bees who make it, and is also on the vegan list of don'ts.

So what *do* vegans eat? Basically, they eat plant-derived foods. Vegetables, fruits, grains, seeds and nuts are central to the vegan diet, and from them come a surprising variety of tasty, nutritious and often ingenious meals. From soya beans come tofu, and soy milk. From sesame seeds comes tahini, from chickpeas hummus. Nuts can be eaten as snacks, as part of savoury dishes or dessert, or they can be made into non-dairy milks. Oats and other grains, preferably wholegrains, can be made into flour, bread, breakfast cereals etc. Substitute eggs for baking can be made from ground flax seeds and water. Delicious ice cream can be made from frozen bananas. And so on.

WHY EAT VEGAN?
People approach veganism from all sorts of directions. The most common is probably from the issue of animal cruelty - the exploitation and killing of animals to provide for our needs, when we already have an abundance of plant life to feed us.

There is also the broader environmental argument, which refutes the old accusations that vegetarians and vegans care more for animals than people. The Vegan Society statement of purpose in 1962 said:

> *Veganism remembers man's responsibilities to the earth and its resources and seeks to bring about a healthy soil and plant kingdom and a proper use of the materials of the earth.*

So, the principles behind veganism encompass the whole planet, from the harmful gasses produced by animal waste, to the belief that we could easily grow enough food to feed the entire world if we didn't have to spend so much of it feeding animals for us to consume. Basically, we cut out the middle man and eat directly what we grow.

Other people come to veganism for health reasons: the harmful effects of meat-based diets and processed foods, and the benefits of fresh, often raw, vegetables and fruit. Many people notice they feel better and have more energy on this lighter, plant-based diet.

Which brings us to weight loss. Cutting out meat, animal fats and dairy produce can help people to lose weight and to stick with the body shape and mass that suits them best.

This book of calorie counted vegan recipes is specifically designed to help with weight loss and the maintenance of your ideal weight, while paying attention to the unique nutritional needs of vegans.

HOW TO EAT VEGAN
To be healthy, you can't simply cut all animal based foods from your diet. You have to pay attention to what you eat and make sure you still get all the nutrients your body needs. For example, several vegans in the 1950s who'd been vegans for more than five years, became ill and listless through what we now know was a deficiency of Vitamin B12. Today most soya milks and nut milks are fortified with Vitamin B12. So are many breakfast cereals. Nutritional yeast, a deactivated, cultured yeast which imparts a cheesy, nutty flavour to food, is another excellent source of this and other vital vitamins.

Other important nutrients that vegans are liable to run short of are protein, calcium, iron and omega 3, all of which can be found in natural plant-based foods and in fortified cereals and milks.

For example, kale, hemp seeds, nuts, tofu, quinoa, lentils and beans are all good sources of protein.

Calcium can be derived from green vegetables such as broccoli and kale, from fennel, sesame seeds, and from fruits such as oranges and blackcurrants and apricots – including the dried varieties.

Good sources of iron are sesame and pumpkin seeds, nuts (especially cashews), beans, whole grains such as quinoa, barley, oats, rice and bulgur, tofu, dried fruit, dark chocolate (yay!) and cocoa powder.

Omega 3, an essential fat, is found in walnuts, chia seeds, flax seeds and hemp seeds, as well as in leafy greens such as cabbage, broccoli and kale, in cauliflower, beans, berries, cloves, mangoes and melons.

Clearly, then, with a little effort, it is quite easy to eat a healthy and balanced vegan diet. The recipes in this book pay particular attention to the variety of vegan nutritional needs.

HOW TO LOSE WEIGHT AS A VEGAN
Whether you're a vegan already and wish to lose a few pounds, or whether you've decided a vegan diet is the best way for you to achieve your body-weight goals, you need to count your calories. All the recipes in this book have been calorie counted for you. With a variety of recipes for each meal and even for between-meal snacks, you should be able to keep within your calorie goal and maintain a healthy, balanced diet.

One of the problems faced by vegans, especially those trying to lose weight, is that of feeling "full" enough after a meal to stop eating. In this cookbook you'll find both light recipes, and those that feel bulkier and keep you satisfied for longer.

Even better, you don't have to give up sweet food or chocolate! A little is good for you, satisfies the sweet craving and most importantly keeps you happy. The recipes in this book are all fun and flavourful, so whether you're looking to cook for yourself or for a party, there is plenty here to tempt you and keep you to your diet! Try it and see.

While all ingredients in our recipes use vegan ingredients, when cooking ensure all your ingredients are vegan-certified by checking the food labels.

breakfast

ᵛ

ALMOND AND RASPBERRY

362 calories per serving

Ingredients

- 75g/3oz raspberries
- 1 medium banana, sliced
- 120ml/4floz unsweetened almond milk
- 1 tbsp sliced almonds
- ¼ tsp ground cinnamon
- Pinch tsp ground cardamom
- Drop of vanilla extract
- 25g/1oz blueberries
- 1 tbsp coconut flakes

Method

1 Add everything, except the blueberries, half the almonds and half the coconut flakes, to your blender.

2 Blend until smooth.

3 Pour the mixture into a bowl and scatter on the blueberries and the remaining almonds and coconut.

CHEFS NOTE

Almond milk contains no cholesterol or saturated fats.

NUTTY BREAKFAST MUFFINS

225
calories per serving

Ingredients

- 150g/5oz muesli
- 50g/2oz light brown sugar
- 165g/5½oz plain flour
- 1 tsp baking powder
- 250ml/1 cup sweetened soy milk

- 1 apple, cored, peeled & grated
- 2 tbsp grapeseed oil
- 3 tbsp peanut butter
- 4 tbsp demerara sugar
- 50g/2oz pecan nuts, chopped

Method

1 Heat the oven to 400F/200C/Gas6.

2 Line a muffin tin with cases.

3 In a bowl, mix about two thirds of the muesli with the light brown sugar, flour and baking powder.

4 In a jug, stir together the milk, apple, oil and 2 tbsp of the peanut butter. When combined stir into the muesli mixture.

5 Divide the mixture between the cases. Then combine the remaining muesli with the demerara sugar, the rest of the nut butter and the pecans. Spread it over the tops of the muffins.

6 Bake in the oven for about half an hour, until the muffins are risen and golden brown.

CHEFS NOTE
Feel free to use almond or other nut butter instead of peanut. The muffins will keep for up to 3 days in an airtight container. Alternatively, you can store them in the freezer for one month.

APRICOT AND OATS

350
calories per serving

Ingredients

- 40g/1½oz rolled oats
- 75ml/2½floz coconut milk
- Pinch salt

- 60g/2½oz dried apricots
- 1 tbsp hazelnuts, chopped
- 1 tsp maple syrup

Method

1 The night before, mix together the oats, coconut milk and salt. Cover and refrigerate overnight.

2 In the morning gently warm the oat mixture on the hob or in the microwave.

3 Scatter the apricots, hazelnuts and maple syrup over the top, and serve.

CHEFS NOTE

Oats are a good source of protein and minerals.

KALE, TOFU AND SWEET POTATOES

265 calories per serving

Ingredients

- 1 small sweet potato, peeled & cubed
- 1 tbsp canola oil
- ½ small onion, chopped
- 375g/13oz tofu, crumbled
- ¼ tsp garlic powder
- 1 tsp ground cumin
- ½ tsp salt
- ¼ tsp turmeric
- 50g/2oz kale
- Salt & pepper to taste

Method

1 Place the sweet potato into a large pan, and cover with water. Bring to the boil, then reduce the heat and simmer for three minutes.

2 Drain the potatoes then add the oil and the onions. Sauté on a medium heat for around 7 minutes. Add the tofu, garlic powder, cumin, salt, and turmeric. Cook for about 5 minutes, stirring frequently.

3 Add the kale, then cover and reduce the heat. Cook for a few minutes until the kale is tender.

CHEFS NOTE
An excellent source of both protein and calcium, this dish can easily be flung together the night before and reheated in the morning.

BANANA & PASSIONFRUIT PANCAKES

175 calories per serving

Ingredients

- 150g/5oz plain flour
- 2 tsp baking powder
- 3 tbsp caster sugar
- 400ml/14floz coconut milk
- Vegan cooking oil spray
- 2 medium bananas, sliced thinly
- Pinch salt
- 2 passion fruits, flesh scooped out

Method

1 Sift the flour and baking powder into a bowl, and stir in 2 tbsp of the sugar and a pinch of salt. Gradually stir ¾ of the coconut milk into the flour mixture to make a smooth batter. Or use a blender, if you prefer.

2 Heat a frying pan and spray it with oil. Drop 2 tbsp of batter into the frying pan for each pancake. You should be able to cook 2 pancakes at a time. Squash about 4 slices of banana into each pancake and cook until the edges are dry and bubbles start to form on the surface. Turn them carefully and cook the other sides for 1 minute. Repeat until all the batter is used.

3 Meanwhile, heat the remaining coconut milk and sugar in a small pan. Season with salt and simmer until the mixture thickens like cream.

4 When your pancakes are ready, pour the coconut milk sauce over and top with the passion fruit.

CHEFS NOTE

These pancakes are a little more delicate than those made with egg batter, so be careful when turning them!

CHIA, APPLE & CINNAMON BREAKFAST

235 calories per serving

Ingredients

- 120ml/4floz unsweetened almond milk
- 2 tbsp chia seeds
- 2 tsp maple syrup
- ¼ tsp vanilla extract
- ¼ tsp ground cinnamon
- 1 apple, peeled and chopped
- 1 tbsp toasted pecans, chopped

Method

1 In a bowl, stir together the almond milk, chia seeds, maple syrup, vanilla and cinnamon. Cover and chill in the fridge for at least 8 hours.

2 When you wish to serve, stir the mixture well. Spoon about half into a serving bowl, and scatter over half the apple and pecans.

3 Layer on the rest of the chia mixture and top with the remaining apple and pecans.

CHEFS NOTE
Chia seeds are a great source of Omega 3.

CAULI-OATS

360 calories per serving

Ingredients

- 650g/1lb7oz cauliflower, broken into florets
- ½ medium banana
- 250ml/9floz unsweetened soy milk
- ½ tbsp almond butter
- 2 tsp maple syrup
- 1½ tsp ground cinnamon
- Pinch salt
- ½ tsp vanilla extract
- 4 strawberries, sliced
- ¼ pear, sliced
- 1 tbsp raw almonds, sliced

Method

1 Place the cauliflower into your food processor and process to make small rice-like granules.

2 Add the banana and process again to mash.

3 Transfer the mixture to a small pan. Pour in the soy milk and add the almond butter, maple syrup, cinnamon, salt, and vanilla. Bring to a simmer for about 12 minutes or until the cauliflower rice is tender and the liquid is absorbed.

CHEFS NOTE
This delicious breakfast looks like porridge, but is both lower in calories and higher in fibre and protein than a bowl of oats.

MAPLE SYRUP AND BLUEBERRY TOAST

218 calories per serving

Ingredients

- 3 tbsp maple syrup
- 150g/5oz blueberries
- 2 tbsp chickpea (gram) flour
- 2 tbsp ground almonds
- 2 tsp cinnamon
- 250ml/8½floz oat milk

- 1 tbsp caster sugar
- 1 tsp vanilla extract
- 6 slices bread
- 3 tbsp grapeseed oil
- Icing sugar, for dusting

Method

1 In a small pan, gently heat the maple syrup and blueberries until the fruit starts to burst, then remove the pan from the heat and set aside.

2 In a shallow bowl, whisk together the flour, almonds, cinnamon, milk, sugar and vanilla.

3 Heat a little of the oil in a frying pan. Dip a slice of bread into the milk mixture, drip off any excess and fry the bread on both sides until golden brown and crispy at the edges. Keep warm while you cook the rest.

4 Scatter the blueberries over the toast and top with a light dusting of icing sugar.

CHEFS NOTE

Oat milk is higher in protein than some non-dairy alternatives, but it does contain more sugar and calories. Try with other milks if you prefer.

QUINOA AND PEACH PORRIDGE

232 calories per serving

Ingredients

- 250ml/8½floz water
- 250ml/8½floz unsweetened almond milk
- 75g/3oz quinoa
- 25g/1oz porridge oats

- 4 cardamom pods
- 2 ripe peaches, stoned and sliced
- 1 tsp maple syrup

Method

1 In a small pan, heat the water and 100ml/3½floz of the almond milk. Add the quinoa, oats and cardamom pods. Bring to the boil and simmer for 15 minutes, stirring occasionally.

2 Pour in the rest of the almond milk and cook for another 5 minutes, until the mixture is creamy.

3 Remove the cardamom pods, then spoon into bowls. Top with the peach slices and maple syrup, and serve.

CHEFS NOTE
Quinoa is one of those rare plants that contains all nine essential amino acids.

CHIA AND GINGER BREAKFAST

310 calories per serving

Ingredients

- 40g/1½oz chia seeds
- 175ml/6floz unsweetened soy milk
- 1 tbsp maple syrup
- ¼ tsp ground ginger
- ¼ tsp cinnamon
- Pinch ground cloves
- Pinch salt
- 1 tbsp raisins
- 1 tbsp pecan nuts, chopped

Method

1 In a bowl, stir together all the ingredients except the raisins and nuts. Chill in the fridge overnight, or for at least 6 hours.

2 When you're ready to eat, scatter on the raisins and nuts to serve.

CHEFS NOTE
Feel free to use other non-dairy milk if you prefer, and swap the pecans for any nut you like.

BREAKFAST SMOOTHIE BOWL

340
calories per serving

Ingredients

- 1 large banana, peeled
- 100g/3½oz frozen mixed berries
- 120ml/4floz unsweetened soy milk
- 50g/2oz pineapple chunks
- ½ kiwi, peeled and sliced
- 1 tbsp almonds, sliced
- 1 tbsp coconut flakes
- 1 tsp chia seeds

Method

1 Blend the banana, berries and soy milk together until smooth.

2 Pour into a bowl and scatter on the pineapple chunks, kiwi slices, almonds, coconut flakes & chia seeds.

3 Serve and enjoy!

CHEFS NOTE

Among other benefits, pineapple is high in Vitamin C, manganese and other antioxidants.

SERVES 2

PROTEIN BREAKFAST BALLS

280
calories per serving

Ingredients

- 75g/3oz rolled oats
- 1 scoop vegan vanilla protein powder
- 1 large banana

Method

1 Tip the oats and protein powder into a food processor.

2 Pulse until the oats are chopped but not completely smooth.

3 Add the banana and pulse again until the mixture becomes a dough.

4 Shape the dough into 12 balls and store them in an airtight container in the fridge until you're ready to eat.

CHEFS NOTE
A simple, tasty way to stay stocked up on protein and energy.

APPLE PANCAKES

172 calories per serving

Ingredients

- 225g/8oz whole-wheat flour
- 2 tsp baking powder
- ¼ tsp salt
- 360ml/12½floz unsweetened almond milk
- 60g/2½oz unsweetened apple sauce

- 2 tbsp coconut oil, melted
- 1 tbsp sugar
- 1 tsp vanilla extract
- Cooking oil spray

Method

1 In a large bowl, combine the flour, baking powder and salt. In another bowl, whisk together the milk, apple sauce, oil, sugar and vanilla. Make a well in the centre of the flour mix, and pour in the milk mixture. Whisk until combined. Set the batter aside for 15 minutes.

2 Spray a large pan or griddle with non-stick cooking oil and heat on medium.

3 Without stirring the batter, drop about 4 tbsp per pancake into the frying pan or griddle. Cook for about 3 minutes, until the edges are dry and bubbles form on the surface, then turn them and cook for another couple of minutes, until they're golden brown on both sides.

4 Remove the pancakes and keep warm while you repeat the process until the batter is used up. Serve with your favourite toppings.

CHEFS NOTE

This recipe should make 12 vegan pancakes, and allows 2 per serving.

APPLE AND CINNAMON GRANOLA

440 calories per serving

Ingredients

- 400g/14oz jumbo oats
- 2 tsp cinnamon
- 150g/5oz dried apple, chopped
- 150g/5oz coconut oil, melted
- 250g/9oz mixed nuts, chopped
- 100ml/3½floz maple syrup

Method

1 Heat the oven to 180C/350F/Gas4. Line two baking trays with parchment.

2 In a bowl, mix together all the ingredients except the maple syrup. Spread the mixture out on the trays and drizzle the maple syrup over the top.

3 Bake in the oven for 20 minutes. After 10, stir the granola so that it cooks evenly.

4 Remove from the oven and allow to cool before storing in an airtight container.

CHEFS NOTE

Oats are incredibly nutritious, and are higher in protein than any other grain. They keep you feeling fuller for longer and therefore aid weight-loss.

lunch

HUMMUS AND AVOCADO TOAST

428 calories per serving

Ingredients

- 75g/3oz rocket
- 1 tsp red-wine vinegar
- 1 tsp extra-virgin olive oil
- 2 slices sprouted whole-wheat bread, toasted
- 50g/2oz hummus
- Salt & pepper
- 25g/1oz bean sprouts
- ¼ avocado, sliced
- 2 tsp sunflower seeds

Method

1 In a bowl toss the rocket with the vinegar, oil, salt and pepper.

2 Spread each slice of toast with 2 tbsp of hummus. Scatter on the beansprouts, avocado slices and rocket. Sprinkle the sunflower seeds over the top and serve.

CHEFS NOTE

Flour made from sprouted grains provides more protein, vitamins and minerals than refined flours.

VEGAN PITTA BURGERS

201 calories per serving

Ingredients

- 400g/14oz tinned chickpeas, rinsed & drained
- 1 small red onion, peeled & roughly chopped
- 1 clove garlic, peeled & crushed
- 1 tbsp freshly chopped flat leaf parsley
- 1 tsp ground cumin
- 1 tsp ground coriander
- ½ tsp harissa paste
- 2 tbsp plain flour
- Pinch salt
- 2 tbsp sunflower oil
- 4 pitta breads, toasted
- 200g/7oz tub tomato salsa, to serve
- Green salad, to serve

Method

1 Pat the chickpeas dry with kitchen towel. Tip them into a food processor and add the onion, garlic, parsley, spices, harissa paste and flour.

2 Season with a little salt. Pulse until smooth-ish then shape into four round burgers with your hands.

3 Heat the oil in a non-stick frying pan. Fry the burgers for around 3 minutes on each side, until they're golden.

4 Serve in toasted pitta bread, garnished with tomato salsa and a green salad.

CHEFS NOTE
Chickpeas are a great source of calcium, iron and protein.

CHICKPEA SALAD

290 calories per serving

Ingredients

- 300g/11oz cherry tomatoes
- 75g/3oz canned chickpeas
- 150g/5oz cucumber, sliced
- 1 tbsp freshly chopped flat leaf parsley
- 1 red onion, peeled & finely chopped

- 2 tbsp extra-virgin olive oil
- 1½ tbsp fresh lemon juice
- ½ tsp black pepper
- ½ tsp salt

Method

1 Halve the tomatoes. Drain and rinse the chickpeas.

2 Add all the ingredients into a bowl.

3 Toss gently to combine, and serve.

CHEFS NOTE

This simple salad is both tasty and nutritious. As well as the all-round goodness of chickpeas, the parsley will give your iron intake an additional boost.

QUINOA WITH SPICED LENTILS

380
calories per serving

Ingredients

To make the quinoa:
- 200g/7oz grams dried quinoa
- 600ml/1 pint vegetable stock
- 2 carrots, peeled and diced
- 400g/14oz tinned black beans
- Salt & pepper

To make the lentils:
- 1 tbsp olive oil

- 1 medium onion, peeled & diced
- 125g/4oz tomatoes, chopped
- 225g/8oz dried green lentils
- 1lt/1½pints vegetable stock
- 6 stalks celery, sliced
- 4 carrots, peeled and chopped
- ¼ tsp ground coriander
- ¼ tsp ground cumin
- Salt & pepper

Method

1 In a pan, heat the quinoa and vegetable stock and bring them to the boil.

2 Reduce the heat and simmer for 10 minutes. Stir in the carrots and beans. Cook for another 20 minutes, until the quinoa fluffs with a fork.

3 Meanwhile, in a larger pan, gently fry onions in olive oil for about 5 minutes. Add the tomatoes, lentils, vegetable stock, celery, carrots, and spices. Cover and cook for an hour, or until the lentils are soft.

4 Spoon the quinoa mixture into bowls, and top with the lentil mixture. Serve at once.

CHEFS NOTE
Lentils are a great source of both iron and protein.

VEGETABLE WRAP

286 calories per serving

Ingredients

- 1 medium carrot, grated
- ½ red cabbage, shredded
- 2 spring onions, thinly sliced
- 1 medium courgette, grated
- Handful basil leaves

- 5 green olives, pitted and halved
- ½ tsp English mustard powder
- 2 tsp extra virgin olive oil
- 1 tbsp cider vinegar
- 1 large seeded tortilla

Method

1 In a bowl, combine all the ingredients except the tortilla. Toss well.

2 Lay the tortilla on a sheet of foil and pile the filling along one side of it. Roll the tortilla from the filling side, folding in the edges as you go. Fold the foil in at the ends to keep stuff inside the wrap.

3 Cut in half and eat immediately.

CHEFS NOTE

Cabbage is rich in vitamins, fibre, calcium, iron and protein.

SCRAMBLED TOFU

105 calories per serving

Ingredients

- Small knob non-dairy butter
- 450g/1lb tofu, drained
- ¼ tsp sea salt
- ½ tsp onion powder
- ½ tsp garlic powder
- ¼ tsp ground turmeric
- 3 tbsp vegetable stock
- Salt & pepper to taste

Method

1 Melt the butter in non-stick pan. Add the tofu, salt and spices.

2 Chop up the tofu as it cooks, so that it looks like scrambled eggs.

3 Gradually add the vegetable stock and bring to the boil, allowing the tofu to fully absorb the stock.

4 Remove from heat and season with sea salt and pepper.

5 Serve and enjoy!

CHEFS NOTE

Tofu is high and protein. Cooking it in stock gives it a delicious flavour. Enjoy with a slice of toast for lunch.

CARROT AND TAHINI SOUP

270
calories per serving

Ingredients

- 1 tbsp olive oil
- 1 large onion, peeled & chopped
- ½ tsp salt
- ½ tsp smoked paprika
- ¼ tsp ground turmeric
- 2 cloves garlic, peeled and finely chopped

- 450g/1lb carrots, peeled and chopped
- 750ml/1¼pints vegetable stock
- 3 tbsp tahini paste
- 2½ tbsp tahini sauce
- 6 tbsp pistachio nuts, coarsely chopped
- 2 tsp fresh oregano leaves, chopped

Method

1 Heat the oil in a large pan and sauté the onion for about 5 minutes.

2 Stir in the salt, paprika, turmeric, and garlic. Cook for a minute, then add the carrots. Cook for another minute before stirring in the stock. Bring to the boil, then reduce the heat, cover and simmer for about 20 minutes, or until the carrots are very tender.

3 Blend the carrot soup with the tahini paste until smooth.

4 Divide the soup into bowls. Drizzle a little tahini sauce over each and then scatter with pistachios and oregano.

CHEFS NOTE

Tahini is made from sesame seeds which are very nutritious. Among other things, they are a good source of calcium.

STUFFED PEPPERS

312 calories per serving

Ingredients

- 600ml/1 pint vegetable stock
- 165g/5½oz quinoa
- 4 large red peppers, halved & de-seeded
- Grapeseed oil for brushing
- 120ml/4floz salsa, plus more for serving
- 2 tsp ground cumin

- 1½ tsp chili powder
- 1½ tsp garlic powder
- 400g/14oz tinned black beans, drained & rinsed
- 165g/5½oz sweetcorn
- Salt & pepper to taste

Method

1 In a pan, bring the vegetable stock and quinoa to the boil.

2 Lower the heat, cover, and simmer for around 20 minutes, until all the liquid is absorbed and the quinoa is fluffy.

3 Meanwhile, preheat the oven to 190C/375F/Gas5 and lightly grease a baking dish or tray. Place the halved peppers in the dish and brush them with grape seed oil.

4 When the quinoa is cooked, tip it into a large mixing bowl. Throw in all the remaining ingredients and mix thoroughly. Adjust the seasoning and spices if desired.

5 Stuff the halved peppers with quinoa mixture until they're full, then cover the dish with foil.

6 Bake in the oven for 30 minutes, then remove the foil, and bake for another 15 minutes or so, until peppers are soft and slightly golden.

CHEFS NOTE
Quinoa adds protein to this delicious lunch dish.

BUCKWHEAT AND TOFU SALAD

296 calories per serving

Ingredients

- 75g/3oz tofu, cubed
- ½ tsp olive oil
- 1 medium carrot, sliced
- 1 medium tomato, sliced
- 1 medium cucumber, sliced
- 25g/1oz fennel, sliced
- 50g/2oz avocado, cubed
- 75g/3oz lettuce
- 1 olive, sliced
- 75g/3oz buckwheat groats, cooked & drained

Method

1 Preheat the oven to 375F/190C/Gas5.

2 Mix the tofu with the olive oil, then tip it onto a baking tray and bake in the oven for 20 minutes. Add the vegetables & cooked buckwheat into a bowl.

3 Chop the tofu into smaller slices and add it to the bowl.

4 Combine well, serve and enjoy!

CHEFS NOTE
Lots of goodness in this salad, and the buckwheat and tofu will keep you feeling full as well as healthy!

BLACK BEAN AND MANGO SALAD

342 calories per serving

Ingredients

- Zest and juice of 1 lime
- 1 small mango
- 1 small avocado
- 100g/3½oz cherry tomatoes
- 1 red chilli

- 1 red onion, peeled and chopped
- 15g/½oz fresh coriander, chopped
- 400g/14oz tinned black beans, drained & rinsed

Method

1 Peel, stone and cube the mango and avocado.

2 Halve the tomatoes. Deseed & chop the chilli.

3 In a bowl, combine the lime zest and juice, mango, avocado, tomatoes, chilli and onion. Gently stir in the coriander and beans.

4 Serve immediately.

CHEFS NOTE
Black beans are high in protein and contain no fat.

VEGETABLE GAZPACHO

240 calories per serving

Ingredients

- 2 slices French bread, crusts removed, torn into small pieces
- 250ml/8½floz water
- Vegan cooking oil spray
- 3 spring onions, trimmed
- 900g/2lb yellow tomatoes, quartered
- 5 tbsp extra-virgin olive oil
- 2 tbsp sherry vinegar
- 1 tbsp tomato paste
- 1½ tsp grated fresh ginger
- 1 tsp salt
- 5 garlic cloves, peeled
- 1 serrano chilli, seeded
- 100g/3½oz red tomato, chopped
- 100g/3½oz green tomato, chopped
- 100g/3½oz courgette, finely chopped
- 1 tbsp chopped fresh coriander leaves

Method

1 Soak the bread in the water for about 10 minutes.

2 Spray a small frying pan with non-stick oil and fry the spring onions for about a minute on each side, until softened. Roughly chop.

3 Blend together the bread mixture, yellow tomatoes, 3 tbsp of the olive oil, vinegar, tomato paste, ginger, salt garlic and chilli.

4 When smooth, pour it into a large bowl. Stir in the spring onions, red tomato, green tomato, courgettes, and about half the coriander.

5 Cover and chill in the fridge for at least 1 hour.

6 Stir well before serving. Drizzle the remaining oil over each bowl and scatter the rest of the coriander over the top.

CHEFS NOTE

Coriander is a good source of vitamins and iron.

VEGAN VARIETY PLATE

495
calories per serving

Ingredients

- 225g/8oz extra-firm tofu, cubed
- 1 tbsp olive oil
- 1 tbsp soy sauce
- Pinch dried basil
- Pinch dried oregano
- 250g/9oz brown rice, cooked

- 1 tbsp miso paste
- ½ head broccoli, cut into florets & cooked
- ½ medium sweet potato, cooked & diced
- 1 large carrot, grated
- 1 tsp sauerkraut
- 1 tsp pickled ginger

Method

1 Heat the olive oil in a pan. Throw in the tofu, basil and oregano. Add the soy sauce and cook on medium heat until the tofu is browned.

2 Mix together the rice and miso paste and tip onto a serving platter. Arrange the tofu mixture, the broccoli, sweet potato, carrot, sauerkraut, and pickled ginger beside it.

3 Serve and enjoy.

CHEFS NOTE

There's a little of everything in this tasty lunch! Broccoli is a good source of iron.

POLENTA WITH BEANS AND TOMATO

286 calories per serving

Ingredients

- 1 tsp olive oil
- 900g/2lb polenta
- 2 cloves garlic, peeled and crushed
- 400g/14oz tinned black beans, rinsed & drained
- 2 x 400g/14oz tins chopped tomatoes
- 1 red pepper, deseeded & diced
- 350g/12oz frozen sweetcorn
- ½ tsp Cayenne pepper
- Salt & pepper to taste

Method

1 Heat the olive oil in a large pan.

2 Cut the polenta into half-inch-size slices. Fry them in the pan until they're brown on each side. Keep them warm while you cook the rest.

3 Meanwhile, add the garlic, beans, tomatoes, red pepper, corn, and spices into another pan. Cook uncovered on medium heat for about 20 minutes.

4 Arrange 4 slices of polenta on each plate and spoon on the vegetable mixture.

5 Serve and enjoy.

CHEFS NOTE
Polenta, like black beans, is low in fat and high in protein.

SERVES 1

GREEN VEGETABLE RICE

329
calories per
serving

Ingredients

- 75g/3oz brown basmati rice
- 140g/4½oz green beans
- ½ small cucumber, finely diced
- 5 spring onions, sliced
- 1 tbsp chopped fresh mint
- Juice of ½ lemon

- 1 cooked beetroot, diced
- 1 small apple, cored and diced
- 1 small red onion, peeled & finely chopped
- 25g/1oz walnuts, roughly chopped
- 1 tbsp balsamic vinegar

Method

1 Boil the rice for 20 minutes, then add the green beans and cook for another 5 minutes, until both are just tender. Drain and leave to cool slightly before stirring in the cucumber, spring onions, mint and lemon juice.

2 Meanwhile, in a bowl, stir together the beetroot, apple, onion, walnuts and balsamic.

3 Spoon the rice onto plates and serve with the salsa. Sprinkle with a few extra mint leaves.

CHEFS NOTE
Walnuts are an important source of omega 3, and go beautifully with this dish.

TOFU SAAG

208
calories per serving

Ingredients

- 600g/1lb5oz firm tofu, cubed
- 2 tbsp canola oil
- 275g/10oz spinach, stems removed
- 275g/10oz kale, stems removed
- 1¾ tsp cumin seeds
- 1½ tsp fennel seeds
- 8 cardamom pods

- 6 whole cloves
- 6 dried red chillies
- 2 tbsp grated fresh ginger
- ¾ tsp salt
- 1½ tbsp vegan butter
- Pinch Cayenne pepper
- 1 tsp water

Method

1 Pat the tofu dry with kitchen towel. Use 1 tbsp of the oil to fry the tofu, in two batches if necessary. Cook for about 4 minutes until golden. Drain the cooked tofu on kitchen towel.

2 Pour about 2 inches of water into a large pan, and bring to the boil. Add the spinach and kale and cover. Cook for about 4 minutes until the leaves have wilted. Drain well, and reserve the cooking liquid. Blend the spinach and kale into a smooth, creamy mixture.

3 Heat the remaining oil in a large pan over medium heat. Add 1 tsp each of cumin seeds and fennel seeds, the cardamom, the cloves and 3 of the chillies. Cook for about 2 minutes, stirring

frequently, until the cumin turns golden brown. Stir in the ginger and cook, stirring, for another half minute. Remove the cloves and cardamom pods with a slotted spoon and discard. Stir in the spinach mixture. Use about 120ml/¼ cup of the spinach cooking liquid to clean out any mixture still clinging to the blender and stir this into the pan too. Add the salt and cook for 5 minutes.

4 Tip the tofu into the pan, cover and cook for 5 minutes.

5 In a small pan, combine the butter with the remaining cumin seeds, fennel seeds, and chillies. Cook for 2 minutes, stirring, until the seeds turn golden brown. Add the Cayenne pepper and water, and then immediately pour the mixture into the big spinach mixture. Stir and serve.

SWEET AND SPICY TOFU

198 calories per serving

Ingredients

- 400g/14oz firm tofu, drained, dried, cubed & thinly sliced
- 3 tbsp chilli-garlic sauce

- 2 tbsp maple syrup
- 2 tbsp reduced-salt soy sauce
- 2 tbsp rice vinegar

Method

1 In a bowl, whisk together the chilli-garlic sauce, maple syrup, soy sauce and rice vinegar. Set aside.

2 Heat a large frying pan on medium-high. Once the pan is thoroughly hot, dry fry the tofu slices in a single layer, in 2 batches if necessary. Cook for 3 to 4 minutes on each side, pressing down with the spatula occasionally, until the tofu is golden brown on each side.

3 Reduce the heat, and with all the tofu in the pan, pour in the prepared sauce. Cook for about 3 minutes, stirring frequently, until the sauce begins to thicken and stick to the tofu.

4 Transfer it all to a bowl and leave to marinate until you're ready to eat. Serve on its own or with rice and vegetables.

CHEFS NOTE
An excellent protein hit! Delicious alone or with brown rice and fresh green vegetables.

BROAD BEAN AND BULGUR SALAD

442 calories per serving

Ingredients

- 50g/2oz bulgur wheat
- 75g/3oz broad beans
- 6 sugar snap peas, halved lengthways
- 4 radishes, thinly sliced
- ½ small red onion, peeled and thinly sliced
- Juice and zest of 1 lime

- ½ small red chilli, deseeded and chopped
- 1 tbsp extra-virgin olive oil
- 1 tsp white wine vinegar
- 1 tsp maple syrup
- Salt & pepper
- 1 tbsp chopped fresh mint leaves

Method

1 Cook the bulgur wheat according to the packet instructions. For the last 3 minutes or so, add the broad beans.

2 Cool under cold running water and drain well. Tip into a serving bowl. Throw in the sugar snap peas, radishes and red onion, and mix well.

3 In a small bowl or jug, whisk together the lime juice and zest, chilli, oil, white wine vinegar and maple syrup. Season with salt and pepper and toss with the salad. Scatter the mint leaves over the top.

CHEFS NOTE
Broad beans are high in protein and fibre, and great for keeping up your energy levels.

CANNELLINI AND KALE SALAD

208
calories per serving

Ingredients

- 3 tbsp olive oil
- 275g/10oz kale, stems removed, shredded
- 400g/14oz tinned cannellini beans, rinsed & drained
- 2 tbsp fresh chopped flat-leaf parsley
- 1 tbsp fresh chopped tarragon
- 1 tsp grated lemon rind
- 1 tbsp lemon juice
- ½ tsp salt
- ¼ tsp black pepper
- 2 cloves garlic, peeled & crushed

Method

1 Heat 2 tsp of the oil in a large pan. Add the kale and cook for half a minute.

2 Stir in the beans and cook for a further minute.

3 In a small bowl, whisk the remaining oil with the rest of the ingredients. Drizzle it over the kale mixture, and serve either warm or chilled.

CHEFS NOTE
Cannellini beans are rich in protein and iron, adding a nutritious burst to this delicious salad.

SPICY CAULIFLOWER AND CHICKPEAS

408 calories per serving

Ingredients

- 1 large head cauliflower, broken into florets
- 2 cloves garlic, peeled & crushed
- 2 tsp caraway seeds
- 2 tsp cumin seed
- 3 tbsp olive oil
- Salt & pepper
- 400g/14oz tinned chickpeas, drained and rinsed
- 100g/3½oz pine nuts
- 1 tbsp fresh chopped flat-leaf parsley
- 2 tbsp fresh chopped dill leaves

Method

1 Heat the oven to 200C/400F/Gas6. In a roasting tin, toss the cauliflower together with the garlic, seeds, and 2 tbsp of the oil. Season with salt and pepper, then roast in the oven for half an hour.

2 Stir in the chickpeas, pine nuts and remaining oil. Return to the oven for another 10 minutes.

3 Stir in the herbs and serve.

CHEFS NOTE

Low in fat and cholesterol, caraway seeds are a good source of calcium, iron and protein.

CAJUN SALAD WITH CROUTONS

334 calories per serving

Ingredients

- 3 tortillas, cut into crouton-sized pieces
- 1 tbsp olive oil
- 1 tsp Cajun seasoning mix
- 1 iceberg lettuce, shredded
- 400g/14oz tinned black beans, rinsed & drained
- 200g/7oz cherry tomatoes, halved
- 2 avocados, stoned, peeled and sliced
- Juice of 1 lime
- 7g/¼oz fresh coriander leaves

Method

1 Pre-heat the oven to 200C/400F/Gas6.

2 Toss the tortilla pieces in the oil and Cajun seasoning, then spread them on a baking tray. Bake in the oven for about 10 minutes until they're crisp.

3 Add the lettuce, beans and tomato to a large bowl. Toss the avocado in the lime juice and add to the salad. Then scatter the tortilla croutons and coriander leaves over the top to serve.

CHEFS NOTE

Avocadoes are rich in vitamins and fibre, but they have 20 times the fat content of other fruits! You can lower the calories of this dish by substituting peaches or apples, but you won't find it so filling.

dinner

v

HOISIN CAULIFLOWER AND TOFU

272 calories per serving

Ingredients

- 350g/12oz firm tofu, drained & cubed
- 3 tbsp cornstarch
- 2 tbsp canola oil
- 250ml/8½floz vegetable stock
- 3 tbsp soy sauce
- 1 tbsp sherry vinegar
- 1½tsp hoisin sauce

- 300g/11oz cauliflower florets
- 200g/7oz celery, thinly sliced
- 6 cloves garlic, peeled and thinly sliced
- 1½ tbsp tomato ketchup
- ½ tsp chilli flakes
- Bunch of spring onions, finely chopped

Method

1 Pat the tofu dry with kitchen towel. Place 2 tbsp of the cornstarch in a large bowl. Add the tofu and toss. Remove the coated tofu from the bowl.

2 Heat the oil in a large pan. Fry the tofu, turning occasionally, for around 6 minutes, until golden and crispy. With a slotted spoon, transfer the tofu to a plate.

3 In a bowl, whisk together the remaining cornstarch with 60ml/2floz of the stock until smooth. Stir in the rest of the stock, the soy sauce, vinegar, and hoisin sauce.

4 Add the cauliflower to the remaining oil in the pan. Cook it, stirring occasionally, for 3 minutes or until

lightly browned. Add the celery and garlic and cook for another 2 minutes. Stir in the ketchup and pepper to coat everything thoroughly. Pour in the stock from the bowl and bring to the boil. Cook for 2 minutes or until the liquid begins to thicken. Stir in the tofu.

5 Serve topped with the spring onions.

CHEFS NOTE

Tofu, high in protein, iron and calcium, is a valuable part of the vegan diet, while cauliflower will boost your omega 3 and fibre intake.

VEGAN CHILLI

270 calories per serving

Ingredients

- 2 tbsp olive oil
- 1 medium onion, peeled & chopped
- 6 cloves garlics, peeled & crushed
- Pinch chilli flakes, to taste
- 1 tbsp chilli powder
- 2½ tsp ground cumin
- 1 tsp dried oregano
- 1 bay leaf
- 2 x 400g/14oz tinned tomatoes
- 1 tbsp soy sauce
- 360ml/12½floz vegetable stock
- 175g/6oz tomato paste
- 1 tbsp red wine vinegar
- 400g/14oz tinned pinto beans, drained & rinsed
- 2 x 400g/14oz tinned kidney beans, drained & rinsed
- Fresh coriander leaves to garnish

Method

1 Heat the oil in a large pan over medium heat and sauté the onion and garlic for about 5 minutes until softened. Add the chilli flakes, chili powder and cumin. Cook for another 2 minutes, then add the oregano, bay leaf, tomatoes, soy sauce, stock, tomato paste, and vinegar.

2 Bring to the boil, the reduce the heat, and simmer for half an hour, stirring occasionally.

3 Add the beans and simmer for a final 15 minutes, or longer if you prefer a softer consistency.

4 Serve scattered with coriander leaves.

CHEFS NOTE

Sprinkle with vegan cheese if desired. The combined kidney beans and pinto beans will top up your protein and iron intake.

TAHINI LENTILS

292
calories per serving

Ingredients

- 50g/2oz tahini paste
- Juice & zest of 1 lemon
- 60ml/2floz cold water
- Salt & pepper
- 2 tbsp olive oil
- 1 red onion, thinly sliced

- 1 clove garlic, peeled & crushed
- 1 yellow pepper, de-seeded & sliced
- 200g/7oz green beans, halved
- 1 courgette, sliced
- 100g/3½oz kale, shredded
- 250g/9oz cooked Puy lentils

Method

1 In a jug, mix the tahini with the lemon juice and zest. Stir in the water. Season to taste, then set aside.

2 Heat the oil in a large frying pan over a medium-high heat. Add the onion and a pinch of salt, and fry for 2 minutes until it begins to soften.

3 Add the garlic, pepper, green beans and courgette and fry for 5 minutes, stirring frequently.

4 Stir in the kale, lentils and the tahini mixture. Cook for a couple more minutes until the kale is wilted.

5 Serve and enjoy!

CHEFS NOTE
Lentils are a great source of fibre, protein and iron.

STUFFED CABBAGE LEAVES IN TOMATO SAUCE

280 calories per serving

Ingredients

- 1 green cabbage
- 1 tbsp olive oil
- 1 onion, peeled and chopped
- 125g/4oz cooked brown lentils
- 175g/6oz cooked quinoa
- 1 tbsp red wine vinegar, plus 1½ tsp

- 2 tbsp soy sauce
- 1 tsp smoked paprika
- Salt & pepper to taste
- 800g/1¾lb tomato passata
- 1 tbsp maple syrup

Method

1 Preheat the oven to 175C/350F/Gas5

2 Boil/steam the cabbage whole in about 3 inches of water.

3 Heat the oil in a large pan. Sauté the onion until translucent. Stir in the cooked lentils, quinoa, 1 tbsp of the red wine vinegar, the soy sauce, smoked paprika, salt & pepper to taste. Remove from the heat.

4 In a bowl, mix together the tomato passata, maple syrup and 1½tsp red wine vinegar. Season and spread about half the sauce into the bottom of a baking dish.

5 Peel a large outer leaf off the cooked cabbage and place it onto your work surface with the stem side towards you. Trim any very thick portions of the leaf. Spoon 3 or 4 tablespoons of the lentil mixture onto the centre of the leaf. Fold the base side over the filling, then wrap the sides inward over the filling. Roll the centre away from you to wrap everything uCabbage will boost your levels of protein, iron and calcium. It's also strong in vitamins.ce the roll, seam side down, into the baking dish. Repeat until all of the filling is used.

6 Pour the remaining sauce over the cabbage rolls, cover and bake in the oven for an hour. Allow them to cool for a few minutes before serving.

SPICY RICE AND VEGETABLE CASSEROLE

280 calories per serving

Ingredients

- 1½ tbsp canola oil
- 1 tsp cumin seeds
- ¼ tsp whole peppercorns
- ¼ tsp cracked peppercorns
- ¼ tsp coriander seeds
- 5 cardamom pods
- 3 whole cloves
- 2 bay leaves
- 1 dried red chilli
- ½ large onion, peeled & sliced
- 1 tsp salt, divided
- 275g/10oz cauliflower florets
- 1 large potato, peeled & diced
- ½ medium sweet potato, peeled & cubed
- ½ tsp ground turmeric
- 225g/8oz basmati rice
- 75g/3oz frozen petit pois
- 500ml/2 cups water
- ½ tsp ground cumin
- ¼ tsp garam masala

Method

1 Heat the oil in a large pan over medium-high heat. Throw in the cumin seeds, peppercorns, coriander seeds, cardamom pods, cloves, bay leaves and chilli. Cook, stirring frequently for a couple of minutes until the cumin browns. Add the onion and ½ tsp salt. Sauté for 2 minutes, then stir in the cauliflower, potatoes, and turmeric. Reduce the heat to medium, and cook for another minute.

2 Add the rice and cook for another minute, stirring occasionally. Stir in the peas and the water. Bring to the boil, then reduce heat further. Stir in the ground cumin, garam masala, and another ½ tsp salt. Cover and cook for 20 minutes.

3 Turn off heat and allow to rest for 5 minutes. Then stir it up, and serve at once.

CHEFS NOTE
Delicious, filling and low in both fat and calories!

BROCCOLI AND BARLEY

380
calories per serving

Ingredients

- 100g/3½oz wholegrain pearl barley
- 1lt/1½ pints water, plus 3 tbsp
- 2 tsp vegetable bouillon powder
- 2 tbsp canola oil
- 1 large leek, chopped

- 2 cloves garlic, peeled
- 50g/2oz basil
- Squeeze lemon juice
- 125g/4oz broccoli, broken into florets

Method

1 Soak the barley overnight in a litre of cold water.

2 Drain the barley, reserve the liquid and use it with the bouillon powder to make 500ml/2 cups vegetable stock.

3 Heat 1 tbsp oil in a pan, and sauté the leek until it softens. Transfer half the leek into a bowl. Add the barley and stock to the rest in the pan. Cover and simmer for 20 minutes.

4 Meanwhile, to the leek in the bowl, add the garlic, basil, remaining oil, lemon juice and 3 tbsp water. Blend to a smooth paste.

5 Tip the broccoli into the pan with the barley and stock, and cook for about 10 minutes more. Stir in the basil purée, heat for another minute, then serve.

CHEFS NOTE
Broccoli and barley provides a great – and tasty! – combination of vitamins, manganese, fibre, omega 3, protein, calcium and iron.

KIDNEY BEAN ENCHILADA

470 calories per serving

Ingredients

- 4 large tortillas
- 1 large onion, peeled & chopped
- 2 large potatoes, peeled & cubed
- 2 medium courgettes, cubed
- 175g/6oz sweetcorn
- 60ml/¼ cup water
- Salt to taste

- 2 tsp Cajun seasoning
- 400g/14oz tinned kidney beans, rinsed & drained
- 50g/2oz fresh coriander, chopped
- 500ml/2 cups enchilada sauce
- 500ml/2 cups tomato sauce

Method

1 Preheat the oven to 190C/375F/Gas5.

2 Heat a large pan on medium. Tip in the onion, potatoes, courgettes and sweetcorn. Pour in the water, and add salt and Cajun seasoning. Bring to the boil, then lower the heat, cover and cook for around 10 minutes, until the potatoes are tender.

3 Stir in the kidney beans, then remove the pan from the heat and stir through the coriander.

4 In a bowl mix together the enchilada and tomato sauce. Spread a thin layer on the bottom of an oven-proof dish.

5 Lay out your tortillas and spread a layer of the enchilada sauce over each.

6 Spread about 4tbsp of the vegetable mixture onto each tortilla and roll it up into a tube shape.

7 Arrange the tortillas, seam down, in the oven-proof dish and pour the remaining sauce over the top. Cover and bake in the oven for about 20 minutes. Uncover and bake on high for another 5 or 10 minutes, until the tortillas are light brown.

CHEFS NOTE

Feel free to swap the kidney beans for another variety you prefer – they're all good for vitamins, fibre, protein and iron.

VEGETABLE AND LEMON STEW

280 calories per serving

Ingredients

- 175g/6oz broad beans
- 60ml/¼ cup olive oil
- 1 medium onion, peeled & sliced
- 75g/3oz fennel bulb, chopped
- ½ medium potato, sliced
- 350g/12oz baby artichokes, halved
- Small bunch spring onions, finely sliced
- ½ tsp fennel seeds, ground

- 4 small carrots, quartered
- 120ml/4floz vegan white wine
- 175ml/6floz water
- Rind from ¼ lemon, cut into strips
- Salt & pepper
- 3 tbsp fresh lemon juice
- ½ tsp cornstarch
- 2 tbsp freshly chopped dill

Method

1 Bring a pan of water to the boil. Tip the beans in and cook them for 1 minute. Drain, then plunge them immediately into ice water. Drain well and set them aside.

2 Heat the oil in a large frying pan over medium heat. Sauté the onions for around 5 minutes, until tender. Add the fennel and potato and cook for another 5 minutes, stirring occasionally. Stir in the artichokes, spring onions, fennel seeds, and carrots.

3 Pour in the wine, water and lemon rind. Season well with salt, and pepper. Reduce the heat and simmer for 10 minutes or so, until the vegetables are tender.

4 In small bowl, stir the lemon juice and cornstarch together until smooth. Stir this mixture into pan. Turn up the heat again and cook for a couple of minutes until the sauce thickens. Stir in the broad beans.

5 Serve scattered with the dill.

CHEFS NOTE

Tasty nutritious and low in calories! The fennel will boost your iron, calcium and protein intake.

TOMATO AND CIABATTA SALAD

330
calories per serving

Ingredients

- 800g/1¾lb tomatoes, roughly chopped
- Salt & pepper
- 1 clove garlic, peeled & crushed
- 1½ tbsp capers, drained & rinsed
- 1 avocado, stoned, peeled & chopped
- 1 red onion, peeled & sliced

- 175g/6oz ciabatta, torn into bite-sized chunks
- 4 tbsp extra virgin olive oil
- 2 tbsp red wine vinegar
- 2 tbsp freshly chopped basil leaves

Method

1 Tip the tomatoes into a bowl and season well. Mix in the garlic, capers, avocado and onion. Set aside.

2 Arrange the ciabatta pieces on a serving platter. Drizzle with 2 tbsp olive oil and 1 tbsp of the vinegar. Season. Pour the tomatoes mix over the top.

3 Sprinkle on the basil leaves and drizzle over the remaining oil and vinegar. Toss and serve at once.

CHEFS NOTE

Capers add a bit of zing to this dish – along with antioxidants, calcium, iron, and very few calories!

AUBERGINE CURRY

240 calories per serving

Ingredients

- 2 large aubergines
- 1 medium onion, peeled & chopped
- ½ red pepper de-seeded & diced
- 1¼ tsp cumin seeds, toasted
- 1¼ tsp ground coriander
- ½ tsp turmeric
- 1 clove garlic, peeled & crushed
- 400g/14oz can chopped tomatoes

- 2 tsp freshly grated ginger
- ½ tsp Cayenne pepper
- 400g/14oz tinned chickpeas, rinsed & drained
- 120ml/4floz water
- 2 tbsp freshly chopped coriander
- ¼ tsp garam masala
- Salt

Method

1 Preheat the oven to 200C/400F/Gas6.

2 Prick the aubergines with a fork and put them on a baking tray. Bake in the oven for around 40 minutes, until sunken and soft all the way through. Remove from oven and leave until cool enough to peel. Once peeled, chop the flesh.

3 Heat a frying pan and dry fry the onion until golden. Add the red pepper, toasted cumin seeds, coriander, turmeric, garlic, tomatoes, ginger and Cayenne pepper.

4 Stir in the aubergine and cook for about 10 minutes. Add the chickpeas and a little water, then cover and simmer on low for at least 15 minutes, stirring occasionally. When the sauce has thickened, stir in the coriander, garam masala, and salt to taste.

CHEFS NOTE

Aubergine is a lovely meaty vegetable that will help fill you up. The chickpeas will add calcium, iron and protein. Serve with wholegrain Basmati rice if you wish.

PEPPER AND QUINOA CHILLI

257 calories per serving

Ingredients

- 2 red peppers, halved & de-seeded
- 2 green chillies, halved & de-seeded
- 4 tsp olive oil
- 3 medium courgettes, chopped
- 2 medium onions, peeled & chopped
- 4 cloves garlic, peeled & crushed
- 1 tbsp chili powder
- 1 tsp ground cumin
- ½ tsp smoked paprika
- 120ml/½ cup water
- 60g/2½oz quinoa
- ¼ tsp salt
- 400g/14oz tinned chopped tomatoes
- 400g/14oz tinned pinto beans, drained and rinsed
- 250ml/8½floz vegetable juice

Method

1 Preheat the grill.

2 Place the pepper and chilli halves flat in the grill pan, skin sides up. Grill until they're blackened, then tip them into a plastic bag and leave them for 10 minutes. They should now peel easily. Chop them roughly.

3 Heat the oil in a large pan over medium-high heat. Throw in the courgette, onion, and garlic and sauté for 5 minutes. Stir in the chilli powder, cumin, and paprika.

4 Add the peppers and chillies. Then stir in the rest of the ingredients and bring to the boil. Lower the heat, cover and simmer for 20 minutes until the quinoa is tender.

5 Serve and enjoy!

CHEFS NOTE

This spicy dish will help boost your levels of protein and iron.

BBQ TOFU

440 calories per serving

Ingredients

- 4 tbsp soy sauce
- 2 tbsp brown sugar
- Pinch ground ginger
- 2 tbsp mirin
- 350g/12oz very firm tofu, drained & thickly sliced

- 3 tsp sesame oil
- ½ tbsp canola oil
- 2 medium courgettes, sliced
- 200g/7oz broccoli, broken into florets
- Handful sesame seeds

Method

1 In a small bowl, combine the soy sauce, sugar, ginger, mirin and 1 tsp of the sesame oil. Brush it all over the tofu slices. Arrange the coated tofu in a shallow dish and pour any leftover soy sauce mixture over the top. Marinate in the fridge for at least an hour, preferably overnight.

2 Meanwhile, stir the canola oil with the remaining sesame oil. Brush the courgette and broccoli with it.

3 When your barbecue is hot enough, cook the courgette and broccoli over it for about 10 minutes, or until they are tender. Transfer them to a serving dish and keep warm.

4 Barbecue the tofu on both sides for around 5 minutes, until it's brown and the edges are crispy. Place the slices on top of the vegetables in the serving dish. Pour the remaining marinade over the top and sprinkle with sesame seeds.

CHEFS NOTE
Tasty, fun and nutritious, with calcium, iron and protein all well covered.

LENTIL BURGERS

290 calories per serving

Ingredients

- 1 tbsp olive oil
- 2 small onions, peeled & chopped
- Pinch salt
- 450g/1lb mushrooms, thinly sliced
- 3 cloves garlic, peeled & crushed
- Freshly ground black pepper
- ½ tsp dried thyme
- ¼ tsp dried tarragon
- 150g/5oz pitted olives
- 250g/9oz cooked lentils
- 125g/4oz breadcrumbs
- 2 tbsp soy sauce
- 2 tsp fresh lemon juice
- Cooking spray

Method

1 Preheat the oven to 175C/350F/Gas4.

2 Heat the oil in a large pan. Sauté the onion for about 3 minutes with a pinch of salt. Throw in the mushroom, garlic, black pepper, thyme and tarragon and cook for another 10 minutes or so, until the mushrooms are cooked.

3 Meanwhile, in your food processor, finely chop the olives and empty them out into a bowl.

4 When the mushroom mixture is cooked, tip it into the food processor. Add all the remaining ingredients except for half the breadcrumbs and the cooking spray. Blend until nearly smooth.

5 Empty the mixture out into a large bowl. Stir in the remaining breadcrumbs and the chopped olives.

6 Divide the mixture evenly into 6 parts and shape each into burgers with your hands.

7 Line a baking tray with parchment paper and coat with cooking spray. Arrange the burgers on the tray and give them a quick spray too. Bake in the oven for 30 minutes, turning them half way through cooking.

CHEFS NOTE

Lentils are rich in protein and iron. For this recipe tinned lentils are best.

COURGETTE NOODLES

190
calories per serving

Ingredients

- 4 small courgettes, processed or spiralized into long noodles
- 1 onion, peeled & diced
- 1 red pepper, de-seeded & chopped
- 3 tbsp vegetable stock
- 1 tbsp garlic powder
- 50g/2oz nutritional yeast
- Salt & pepper

Method

1 Put the courgettes, onion and red pepper into a pan with the vegetable stock. Cook over medium heat for about 3 minutes.

2 Add the garlic powder and nutritional yeast, and cook, stirring occasionally until everything is combined and creamy.

3 Season to taste with salt and pepper and serve.

CHEFS NOTE
Nutritional yeast gives the dish a delicious, cheesy flavour. It's also very low in fat and high in protein and vitamins.

KALE, CHICKPEA AND CASHEW CURRY

290 calories per serving

Ingredients

- 1 large onion, peeled & chopped
- 4 cloves garlic, peeled & chopped
- 1 tbsp freshly grated ginger
- 1 tsp cumin seeds
- 2 tsp garam masala
- 1 tsp ground coriander
- 1 tsp turmeric
- ¼ tsp chilli flakes

- 175g/6oz kale, stems removed
- 120ml/4floz vegetable stock
- 40g/1½oz cashew nuts, raw
- 2 tbsp tomato puree
- 250ml/8½floz unsweetened soy milk
- Salt & pepper
- 2 x 400g/14oz tinned chickpeas, drained & rinsed

Method

1 In a large pan, dry fry the onion for about 4 minutes until it begins to brown. Add the garlic, ginger, and cumin seeds and cook for another minute. Then stir in the garam masala, coriander, turmeric and chilli flakes and cook for a further minute, stirring constantly.

2 Reduce the heat. Pour in the vegetable stock and add the kale. Cover and cook for 5 minutes, stirring occasionally.

3 Meanwhile, blend the cashews, nutritional yeast, and tomato paste with the milk. When the kale is cooked, add that mixture to the blender too and whizz into a smooth puree.

4 Empty the mixture back into the pan and warm to a simmer. Adjust the seasoning. Stir in chickpeas cook for 10 minutes.

CHEFS NOTE

Cashews are low in fibre for nuts, but rich in vitamins, antioxidants and minerals, including iron. Serve with rice if you wish.

CAULIFLOWER CURRY

322 calories per serving

Ingredients

- 1 tbsp olive oil
- 2 cloves
- 4 black peppercorns
- 1 tsp paprika
- 2 tsp curry powder
- 1 tsp turmeric
- ¼ tsp ground cinnamon
- ¼ tsp allspice
- 1 tbsp ground coriander

- 1 red onion, peeled & chopped
- 2 carrots, peeled & chopped
- 1 sweet potato, peeled & chopped
- 4 potatoes peeled & chopped
- 1 red pepper de-seeded & chopped
- 75g/3oz peas
- 2 cloves garlic, peeled & crushed
- 1 tsp freshly grated ginger
- 500ml/2 cups vegetable stock

- 200g/7oz red split lentils
- 400g/14oz tinned chopped tomatoes
- 300g/11oz cauliflower florets
- Salt & pepper
- 1 tbsp fresh coriander, chopped, to garnish

Method

1 Pre-heat the oven to 180C/350FGas4.

2 Heat the oil in a large casserole dish. Fry the spices for one minute, then stir in the onion, carrots, potatoes, red pepper, peas, garlic and ginger. Cook for a minute or two.

3 Add the tomatoes, vegetable stock, and lentils, and bring to the boil. Reduce the heat and simmer for 10 minutes.

4 Transfer the casserole dish to the oven and bake for 30 minutes.

5 Stir in the cauliflower florets, then return to the oven for a further 20 minutes.

6 Adjust the seasoning and serve scattered with the coriander.

CHEFS NOTE

This delicious curry is packed with vitamin C, fibre antioxidants, protein and iron.

SIMPLE VEGETABLE SPAGHETTI

320
calories per serving

Ingredients

- 250g/9oz whole wheat spaghetti (egg-free)
- ½ courgette, chopped
- ½ aubergine, chopped
- 1 medium red onion, peeled & chopped
- 2 cloves garlic, peeled & crushed
- 200g/7oz cherry tomatoes, halved
- 1lt/1½ pints vegetable stock
- 1 tsp dried mixed herbs
- Salt & pepper
- 100g/3½oz broccoli, broken into florets
- 200g/7oz kale, roughly chopped, stems removed

Method

1 Add the spaghetti and all the other ingredients, except the kale and the broccoli, into a large pot. Cook them together for around 6 minutes or so, then add the kale and broccoli.

2 Cook for another 10 minutes until the spaghetti is ready to eat.

3 No need to drain, just serve as is (any remaining stock will add a soupy/ramen like texture).

CHEFS NOTE

Easy, delicious and nutritious! The kale will give you an extra hit of calcium.

CHUNKY WINTER VEGETABLE SOUP

220 calories per serving

Ingredients

- 1 tbsp olive oil
- 1 onion, peeled & chopped
- 2 cloves garlic, peeled & crushed
- 3 parsnips, chopped
- 2 parsnips, grated
- 3 carrots, chopped
- 2 carrots, grated
- 2lt/3 pints vegetable stock
- 1 tsp ground cumin
- 1 tsp dried coriander
- 150g/5oz red lentils, rinsed
- Salt & pepper

Method

1 Heat the oil in a large pan. Add the onions and garlic and sauté until the onions are soft.

2 Add the chopped parsnips and carrots and cook gently for a few minutes more. Pour in the stock and the grated vegetables. Add the cumin, coriander and red lentils.

3 Bring to the boil, stirring occasionally, then lower the heat to simmer, cover and cook for half an hour until the vegetables are soft and the soup lovely and thick.

4 Season with salt and pepper, and ladle into bowls.

CHEFS NOTE

Low in saturated fats, this is a thick, satisfying and nutritious soup to help you enjoy losing weight.

PEPPER PIZZA

225
calories per
serving

Ingredients

- 60ml/2 floz tomato passata
- ½ tsp dried chilli flakes
- 2 cloves garlic, peeled & crushed
- 2 tbsp freshly chopped basil leaves
- 1 large, low-fat tortilla wrap
- 2 tbsp nutritional yeast

- Vegan cooking spray
- ¼ red onion, peeled & sliced
- ¼ courgette, diced
- ½ red pepper, de-seeded & sliced
- ½ green pepper, de-seeded & sliced
- ½ yellow pepper, de-seeded & sliced

Method

1 Preheat the oven to 190C/375F/Gas5.

2 Blend together the passata, chilli flakes, whole garlic clove and basil to make a smooth sauce.

3 Spread 3 tbsp of the sauce on to the tortilla. Sprinkle on the nutritional yeast and spread it around.

4 Coat a frying pan with cooking spray and heat. Sauté the onion, courgette, peppers and crushed garlic until softened.

5 Arrange the vegetables on the wrap, then transfer it to the oven with a spatula.

6 Bake for 10 minutes, or until the edges are golden brown and crispy.

7 Sprinkle some more fresh basil over the top and serve.

CHEFS NOTE
Low in fat and delicious hot or cold, the pizza will keep in the fridge for a couple of days.

RATATOUILLE

216
calories per serving

Ingredients

- 2 tbsp olive oil, plus 1 tsp
- 2 red onions, peeled & cut into wedges
- 4 cloves garlic, peeled & crushed
- 2 aubergines, chopped
- 3 courgettes, chopped
- 3 yellow peppers, de-seeded & chopped
- 6 ripe tomatoes, roughly chopped

- 2 tbsp freshly chopped basil
- Few sprigs fresh thyme
- 400g/14oz tinned chopped tomatoes
- 1 tbsp balsamic vinegar
- Salt and pepper
- Zest of ½ lemon, grated

Method

1 Heat 2 tbsp oil in a large casserole dish, and sauté the aubergines, courgettes and peppers for around 5 minutes, until slightly softened, but not cooked. With a slotted spoon, transfer the veg to a bowl and set aside.

2 Add another tsp oil to the pan, and throw in the onion, garlic, basil stalks and thyme leaves. Fry gently for about 10 minutes, or until softened and golden.

3 Return the cooked vegetables to the pan, then stir in the fresh and tinned tomatoes, and the balsamic. Season with salt and pepper.

4 Cover and simmer for half an hour to reduce the liquid and intensify the flavour.

5 Stir through the basil leaves and lemon zest. Adjust the seasoning and serve.

CHEFS NOTE
This classic dish is delicious with wholegrain rice, vegan-suitable pasta or fresh, crusty bread.

VEGAN
FOOD

desserts

v

CHOCOLATE CHIA DESSERT

198 calories per serving

Ingredients

- 250ml/8½floz soya milk
- 40g/1½oz chia seeds
- 3 tbsp cocoa powder
- 1 tsp vanilla extract

- 1 tbsp freshly squeezed orange juice
- 1 tsp grated orange zest
- 2 tbsp maple syrup

Method

1 In a serving bowl, whisk together all the ingredients until thoroughly combined. Alternatively, for a smoother pudding, blend them.

2 Cover the bowl and chill in the fridge for at least an hour or preferably overnight.

3 If you wish, garnish with chocolate chips, or fruit slices.

CHEFS NOTE
A sweet and delicious way to get the benefits of chia seeds, rich in omega 3, protein and calcium. If you wish substitute a different non-dairy milk for soy.

EASY EGGLESS MERINGUES

38 calories per serving

·········· *Ingredients* ··········

- Aquafaba (liquid) from a 400g/14oz tin of chickpeas
- 100g/3½oz caster sugar

·········· *Method* ··········

1 Heat the oven to 140C/275F/Gas 1 and line a baking tray with parchment.

2 Using an electric mixer or food processor, whisk the chickpea liquid into soft peaks. Gradually add the caster sugar, whisking constantly, until the mixture is thick and silky.

3 Spoon about 12 separate dollops of the mixture onto the baking tray, each about 7 or 8 cm wide. Bake in the oven for approx. an hour or until the meringues are crisp. Allow to cool and serve. Delicious with with strawberries and soya cream.

CHEFS NOTE
These are so low in calories, you can serve them LOADED with soya cream and not feel guilty!

SWEET CARROT AND WALNUT SMOOTHIE

150 calories per serving

Ingredients

- 1 large carrot, peeled and grated
- 8 walnut halves, soaked overnight
- 1 tsp ground cinnamon
- ½ tsp ground mixed spice
- 4 dates, pitted and chopped
- 250ml /1 cup almond milk, or more, if needed
- 1 tsp vanilla extract

Method

1 Blend all the ingredients together until smooth.

2 Adding a little more almond milk if necessary.

3 Pour the smoothie into 2 glasses and serve immediately with crushed ice.

CHEFS NOTE
Smells and tastes like carrot cake! Walnuts are rich in omega 3 and antioxidants.

RASPBERRY & CHOCOLATE MUG CAKE

180 calories per serving

Ingredients

- 1 tbsp ground flax seeds
- 3 tbsp water
- 1 small over-ripe banana
- 3 tsp dark cocoa powder
- 40g/1½oz frozen raspberries
- Granulated sweetener, if desired

Method

1 Make a "flax egg" by whisking together the ground flax seeds and water. Chill in the fridge to set for 15 minutes.

2 When it's ready, drop it into your blender or food processor, together with the banana and cocoa powder. Blend the mixture into a fine batter. Stir in the raspberries.

3 Grease a small dish or mug, and pour in the batter. Cook in the microwave for 60 seconds, or longer for a drier texture.

4 Sprinkle with sweetener if desired, and eat!

CHEFS NOTE
Flax seeds are a good source of omega 3, and make an excellent egg substitute in baking. You can also use chia seeds for this purpose.

MINI CHEESECAKES

326 calories per serving

Ingredients

- 200g/7oz dates, stoned
- 125g/4oz walnuts, shelled
- 175g/6oz cashews nuts, shelled and soaked
- Juice of 1 large lemon
- 75g/3oz coconut oil, melted

- 120ml/4floz full-fat coconut milk
- 120ml/4floz maple syrup
- 40g/1½oz fresh or frozen blackcurrants, blueberries or raspberries

Method

1 In your food processor pulse the dates until they begin to form a sticky lump. Empty out and set aside.

2 Throw in the walnuts and process into a fine meal. Scrape the dates back in and blend with the walnuts nuts to form a loose dough.

3 Lightly grease a 12-cup muffin tin. Dollop a large tablespoonful of the mixture in each cup and press down with your fingers, and then with the back of a spoon or glass to make a packed crust. Put in the freezer for 15 minutes to firm.

4 Meanwhile, blend together the cashews, lemon juice, coconut oil, coconut milk and maple syrup, until silky smooth. Add a little more coconut milk if necessary.

5 Take the muffin tin out of the freezer and spoon the filling evenly over each of the bases. Top with the raspberries or other fruit, then cover the tin with cling-film and freeze for about 5 hours until set hard. Allow them to thaw for ten minutes before serving.

CHEFS NOTE
The nuts in these gorgeous little cheesecakes will boost your omega 3, calcium and protein intake.

RHUBARB AND CUSTARD CAKE

410 calories per serving

Ingredients

- 250g/9oz rhubarb, chopped into 1-inch pieces
- 275g/10oz caster sugar
- 1 tsp vanilla bean paste
- 250g/9oz vegan margarine, plus extra for greasing
- 2 tbsp ground flax seeds
- 6 tbsp water
- 150g/5oz soya custard
- 250g/9oz self-raising flour
- 1 tsp baking powder
- 1 tsp vanilla extract
- 125g/4oz unsweetened apple sauce

Method

1 Pre-heat the oven to 200C/400F/Gas6.

2 Arrange the rhubarb in a roasting tin and combine in a teaspoon of the sugar and all the vanilla bean paste. Shake up the tin to mix then bake in the oven for 15 minutes.

3 Pour away any liquid from the tin and allow the rhubarb to cool.

4 Meanwhile, lower the oven heat to 170C/350F/Gas4. Grease and line a cake tin with parchment.

5 In a bowl, mix the flax seeds with 6 tbsp water. Leave for 5 minutes.

6 In another bowl, whisk together the margarine, 100g/3½oz of the custard, the flour, baking powder, vanilla extract and the remaining sugar. When it's well combined and fluffy, stir in the flax seed mixture and the apple sauce.

7 Pour about a third of the mixture into the cake tin. Layer on a third of the rhubarb, and repeat until you have 3 layers of each. Scatter little dollops of the remaining custard over the top.

8 Bake in the oven for 45 minutes, then cover and bake for another half hour or until golden brown on top and the middle is cooked.

9 Serve warm or cold!

COFFEE AND CHOCOLATE SMOOTHIE

155 calories per serving

Ingredients

- 1 medium frozen banana
- 1 date, stone removed
- 2 tbsp chia seeds
- 120ml/4floz coffee, cold
- 120ml/4floz almond milk
- 2 tbsp unsweetened cocoa powder
- Ice

Method

1 Add all the ingredients into your blender and blend until smooth.

2 Pour into 2 glasses and serve

CHEFS NOTE
Although almond milk is lower in fat and calories than other milks, it also has less protein and calcium so you may wish to choose a variety that is fortified with vitamins and calcium.

EGGLESS ETON MESS

385 calories per serving

Ingredients

- Aquafaba (liquid) from 400g/14oz tin chickpeas
- 100g/3½oz caster sugar
- 500g/1lb2oz mixed berries
- 2 tbsp icing sugar
- ½ tbsp rose water
- 400ml/14floz vegan coconut yogurt

Method

1 Pre-heat the oven to 140C/275F/Gas1 and line a baking tray with parchment.

2 Using an electric mixer or food processor, whisk the aquafaba until white and fluffy. Gradually whisk in the caster sugar until the mixture forms stiff peaks, like making meringues.

3 Spoon the mixture onto the lined baking tray in dollops, and bake in the oven for 1-1½ hours, or until the meringues lift easily off the parchment. Allow them to cool.

4 Meanwhile, in a bowl, mix the berries with the icing sugar and rose water. Leave for half an hour to let the flavours infuse.

5 Pour the yogurt into a large bowl. Crumble the meringues over the top and stir. Then fold in about a third of the berries, to make a ripple effect in the yogurt. Divide the mixture between 4 glass serving dishes. Spoon the remaining berries over the top.

6 Serve at once, or chill in the fridge until you're ready to eat.

CHEFS NOTE
A delicious vegan alternative to the classic – and not too high in calories!

CREAMY PUMPKIN PUDDING

158 calories per serving

Ingredients

- 1 large avocado
- 75g/3oz cooked or tinned pumpkin
- 175g/6oz silken tofu
- 4 dates, stones removed
- 1 tbsp maple syrup
- 1 tsp cinnamon
- Pinch sea salt

Method

1 Peel & stone the avocado.

2 Add all the ingredients to a blender, and blend for several minutes until smooth.

3 Divide the mixture between 4 dishes. Enjoy as it is, or with yogurt, cream, nuts etc.

CHEFS NOTE
Enjoy some extra protein, iron and calcium from the tofu in this yummy dessert.

CHERRY AND CHOCOLATE ICE CREAM

198 calories per serving

Ingredients

- 450g/1lb pitted frozen cherries
- ½ medium banana, frozen
- 120ml/4floz unsweetened almond milk
- 3 tbsp dairy-free chocolate chips

Method

1 Pour half the almond milk into ice cube trays and freeze for at least three hours.

2 In a food processor blend the frozen cherries and banana, the almond-milk ice cubes, and the rest of the almond milk until completely smooth.

3 Stir in chocolate chips, and serve immediately.

CHEFS NOTE
You can either freeze the fruit yourself the night before, or buy it frozen.

PINEAPPLE CREAM

Ingredients

- 400g/14oz frozen pineapple chunks
- ½ frozen banana
- 2 tbsp unsweetened almond milk

Method

1 Blend all the ingredients together to make a smooth cream. You may have to scrape down the sides of your blender occasionally.

2 Pour it into serving dishes and eat!

CHEFS NOTE

Delicious on its own or served with a few chopped nuts or dairy-free chocolate chips.

PINEAPPLE SMOOTHIE

175 calories per serving

Ingredients

- 600ml/1 pint carrot juice, chilled
- 200g/7oz tinned pineapple chunks
- 2 bananas
- ½ tsp freshly grated ginger
- 25g/1oz cashew nuts
- Juice of 1 lime

Method

1 Blend all the ingredients together until smooth.

2 Drink immediately or store in the fridge for a day.

CHEFS NOTE

Delicious, spicy and nutritious!

MANGO & PASSIONFRUIT SMOOTHIE

240 calories per serving

Ingredients

- 250ml/8½floz coconut milk
- 4 tbsp vegan yogurt
- 1 medium banana
- 1 tbsp ground flax seeds
- 125g/4oz frozen mango chunks
- 1 passion fruit, halved, flesh scooped out

Method

1 Blend all the ingredients (except the passionfruit seeds) together until smooth.

2 Pour into 2 glasses and drop the passionfruit seeds on top.

CHEFS NOTE

In this delicious smoothie flax seeds add an omega 3 hit to the fruity goodness

CHOCOLATE HUMMUS

190 calories per serving

Ingredients

- 40g/1½oz almonds
- 5 dates, stones removed
- 400g/14oz can chickpeas, rinsed and drained
- 1 tbsp unsweetened cocoa powder
- 2 tsp maple syrup
- 1 tsp vanilla extract
- ¼ tsp ground cinnamon
- 120ml/4floz vanilla soy milk

Method

1 In a food processor, pulse the almonds for about 5 minutes until they're almond butter. Add all the other ingredients and blend into a puree. Serve at once, on its own or with fruit.

CHEFS NOTE

Chickpeas add calcium, iron and protein to this lovely, mousse-like dessert.

snacks

CRUNCHY CINNAMON AND CHOCOLATE CHICKPEAS

142 calories per serving

Ingredients

- 400g/14oz tinned chickpeas, drained & rinsed
- 2 tsp olive oil
- 2 tbsp cocoa powder
- 3 tsp coconut sugar
- ½ tsp cinnamon
- Pinch salt

Method

1 Preheat the oven to 200C/400F/Gas 6. Line a baking tray with parchment

2 Tip the chickpeas into a bowl and stir in the oil, cocoa powder, coconut sugar, cinnamon, and salt, until the chickpeas are thoroughly coated.

3 Spread the coated chickpeas out on the baking tray and roast in the oven for half an hour, stirring half way through.

4 Allow them to cool for 15 minutes, then tip them into a bowl and serve.

CHEFS NOTE

A lovely crunchy snack to boost your levels of protein, fibre and iron.

SPICY SWEET POTATO WEDGES

152 calories per serving

Ingredients

- 2 large sweet potatoes, cut into wedges
- 2 tbsp olive oil
- 1 tbsp chilli powder
- ½ tsp ground cumin
- ½ tsp garlic powder
- ¼ tsp Cayenne pepper
- 4 tbsp non-fat vegan Greek yogurt
- 2 chillies, finely chopped
- 1 tsp fresh lime juice

Method

1 Preheat the oven to 220°C/425°F/Gas7.

2 In a bowl, mix the olive oil, cumin, chilli powder, garlic powder, and Cayenne pepper. Toss the sweet potato wedges in the mix until they're all thoroughly coated.

3 Tip the coated wedges into a roasting tin and roast them, cut-side down, for half an hour, turning once during cooking.

4 Meanwhile, in a small bowl, mix the yogurt, chillies and lime juice.

5 When the wedges are cooked and crispy, remove them from the oven and serve with the yogurt dip.

CHEFS NOTE

Delicious as a snack on their own, or as an accompaniment to a main meal. Sweet potatoes are also rich in vitamins and minerals and fibre.

RED ONION SHELLS

Ingredients

- 1 red onion
- 1 tbsp peanut butter
- 1 lime
- Chilli powder

Method

1 Cut the onion in half. Peel the layers from the onion halves, half or quarter them again, and use them as tiny dishes.

2 Spread a little peanut butter on each. Sprinkle some lime zest over the top, then dust with chilli powder.

3 Squeeze on some lime juice and enjoy!

CHEFS NOTE
Sweet, tangy and full of protein!

VEGAN MINI QUICHES

36 calories per serving

Ingredients

- Vegan cooking oil spray
- 50g/2oz chickpea (gram) flour
- 175ml/6floz water
- 3 tbsp nutritional yeast
- Pinch salt

- 1 tbsp dried mixed herbs
- 8 sundried tomatoes, chopped
- 2 onions, peeled & chopped
- 2 cloves garlic, peeled & crushed
- Salt & pepper

Method

1 Preheat the oven to 220C/425F/Gas7.

2 Spray an eight hole non-stick muffin tray with cooking oil.

3 In a bowl, whisk together the chickpea flour, water, nutritional yeast, herbs and sun dried tomatoes.

4 Spray a frying pan a little cooking oil and sauté the onion and garlic until softened. Remove from the pan and stir into the chickpea flour mix. Season well.

5 Divide the mixture evenly between the 8 cups in the muffin tin. Bake in the oven for 15 minutes, or until the quiches are firm and browned on top.

6 Serve warm.

CHEFS NOTE
The quiches are quick and easy to make, and are a good source of protein beside. Plus, they make a delicious any-time snack!

ALMOND AND CHIA PROTEIN BARS

284
calories per serving

Ingredients

- 500g/1lb2oz almond butter
- 450g/1lb pure maple syrup
- 100g/3½oz vanilla chai protein powder

- 100g/3½oz vanilla whey protein powder
- 40g/1½oz oats
- 40g/1½oz chia seeds

Method

1 Microwave the almond butter and maple syrup together for 90 seconds. Stir thoroughly and combine with the protein powders, oats & chia seeds.

2 Line a baking tray or other large dish with parchment. Turn the mixture out onto it and spread evenly. Chill in the fridge for at least 4 hours, or preferably overnight.

3 Cut into 16 bars and eat when you wish!

CHEFS NOTE
A fabulous energy-boosting snack, with loads of protein, omega 3 and calcium.

BANANA BOOST

156
calories per
serving

Ingredients

- ½ tbsp peanut butter
- 1 tbsp vanilla protein powder
- Few drops water
- 1 banana, halved lengthwise

Method

1 In a bowl, mix together the peanut butter, protein powder and a few drops of water.

2 Spread the mixture over one half of the banana, and top with the other half.

3 Eat immediately.

CHEFS NOTE
Giving an extra protein kick to the banana's natural energy. Enjoy particularly after a workout.

PISTACHIO NUT BUTTER

89
calories per
tablespoon

Ingredients

- 10 cardamom pods, seeds removed
- 400g/14oz pistachio nuts, shelled
- 1 tbsp maple syrup
- ½ tsp sea salt
- 2 tsp peanut oil

Method

1 Using a mortar and pestle, crush the cardamom seeds as finely as you can.

2 Empty the seeds into your food processor along with the pistachios, maple syrup and salt. Blend into a smooth nut butter. Dribble in a little peanut oil and blend again.

3 Transfer to a jar and enjoy a tablespoon at a time spread on your favourite bread or crispbread.

CHEFS NOTE

Cardamom seeds are loaded with vitamins, calcium and iron.

BANANA TOAST

198 calories per serving

Ingredients

- 1 ripe banana
- 250ml/9oz unsweetened soy milk
- ½ tsp ground cinnamon
- ¼ tsp vanilla extract
- Cooking oil spray
- 2 slices bread, halved

Method

1 Pre-heat a frying pan on the hob, and spray with non-stick oil.

2 In a shallow bowl, mash the banana with the milk, cinnamon, and vanilla until well combined.

3 Dip one half-slice slice of bread at a time into the banana milk mixture to coat thoroughly, then place it in the hot frying pan. You should be able to fry two half-slices at a time. Cook on each side for around 4 minutes, until golden brown. Keep warm while you cook the rest.

4 Serve immediately as is, or with fruit or syrup.

CHEFS NOTE

Soy milk contains less fat than cow's milk but has similarly high calcium and protein content. Some brands are also fortified with vitamins and extra calcium.

ROASTED EDAMAME WITH SESAME SEEDS

150 calories per serving

Ingredients

- 350g/12oz frozen edamame beans, thawed
- 2 tsp olive oil
- 1 tsp sea salt
- 1 tbsp sesame seeds

Method

1 Preheat the oven to 230°C/450°F/Gas8.

2 Pour the edamame into a bowl with the oil and salt. Toss them together to coat the edamame thoroughly.

3 Tip them onto to a baking tray, and bake in the oven for 15 minutes.

4 Scatter the sesame seeds over the top and bake for another 5 minutes.

5 Tip into a bowl and serve.

CHEFS NOTE

Edamame are immature soy beans, steamed in their pods. They are sweeter than mature soy beans but contain all the same nutrients, including protein and calcium. This tasty recipe gives them added crunch!